Write
Reflectively

Sara Miller McCune founded SAGE Publishing in 1965 to support the dissemination of usable knowledge and educate a global community. SAGE publishes more than 1000 journals and over 800 new books each year, spanning a wide range of subject areas. Our growing selection of library products includes archives, data, case studies and video. SAGE remains majority owned by our founder and after her lifetime will become owned by a charitable trust that secures the company's continued independence.

Los Angeles | London | New Delhi | Singapore | Washington DC | Melbourne

SUPER
QUICK
SKILLS

Write
Reflectively

Julian
Edwards

Los Angeles | London | New Delhi
Singapore | Washington DC | Melbourne

Los Angeles | London | New Delhi
Singapore | Washington DC | Melbourne

SAGE Publications Ltd
1 Oliver's Yard
55 City Road
London EC1Y 1SP

SAGE Publications Inc.
2455 Teller Road
Thousand Oaks, California 91320

SAGE Publications India Pvt Ltd
B 1/I 1 Mohan Cooperative Industrial Area
Mathura Road
New Delhi 110 044

SAGE Publications Asia-Pacific Pte Ltd
3 Church Street
#10-04 Samsung Hub
Singapore 049483

Editor: Jai Seaman
Editorial assistant: Rhiannon Holt
Production editor: Nicola Marshall
Proofreader: Sharon Cawood
Marketing manager: Catherine Slinn
Cover design: Shaun Mercier
Typeset by: C&M Digitals (P) Ltd, Chennai, India

Library of Congress Control Number: 2022946122

British Library Cataloguing in Publication data

A catalogue record for this book is available from
the British Library

ISBN 978-1-5297-9080-1 (pbk)

Contents

Everything in this book!

Section 1   What is writing reflectively?

It is your chance to use a learning key to unlock a positive and continuous learning skill at work, university or in your personal life.

Section 2   Why is a reflective learner journal useful?

Use the learner journal template provided in this section to record your learning events and make them memorable. Make notes on your ideas to develop them into themes for writing.

Section 3   How do I prepare for a reflective assignment?

Learn how to check the assignment requirements with a tutor and discuss a research theme to add interest to a personal development project.

Use reflection to link your personal knowledge and experience to an interesting point about a learning event, which you feel needs explaining or understanding. Take a look at some possible themes as a guide.

The session guides in this research plan will get you researching and writing freely and intuitively to process and realize your reflection as a point of action, using supporting academic literature.

Use a generic assignment introduction template to make a rough plan for your first reflective writing draft. Use the plan as a basis for free-writing, thinking and drafting your way to a deadline.

Look at the different styles of writing and argument type and see how you can use critical thinking to support your ideas. Learn about the structure of an argument and get ready to start the final drafting process.

Have I written what I wanted to? Have I missed anything out? Use a checklist, suggested software and a friend to scrutinize your final draft, using the techniques recommended in this section.

After you receive your assignment grade, it is time to reflect on how you did and to recycle your tutor feedback comments into future learning goals. This section shows you how to join a fresh reflective cycle.

What is writing reflectively?

10-second summary

Writing reflectively is a chance to work though the stages of a reflective cycle before, during and after an experience to reflect on academic, professional or personal development goals.

Writing about an experience often makes us think about how we could do better next time, and it helps to explain our feelings about a situation. You will need to think, write and discuss using reflective models, subject theory and multidisciplinary sources from academic literature to create an effective reflective assignment.

Critical incidents and experiences with experts and peers can be turned into memorable learning events by reflecting on academic, work or personal settings and influences.

Experiences may not go the way you planned, but reflecting on unforeseen events with a positive mindset in a written form helps you understand your feelings and change future events. Writing reflectively means you can develop insight from hindsight and create foresight for your learning, work practice or personal change. In this book, you will learn how to write about an experience, create a theme for reflection and link this to a supporting theory, before using different arguments to form a conclusion for future action.

'I only thought I could write about my feelings and impressions of an experience.'

What can I write about?

Essential Questions for a Reflective Assignment

- How did I feel at the time?

- What went well?

- What went badly?

- What would I do differently?

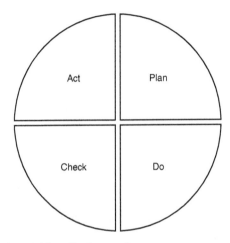

Figure 1.1   A model for reflective practice

Adapted from Moen and Norman (2009)

A reflective cycle illustrates how you **plan** for an event or a design, **do** something or experience the situation, **check** over or reflect on what you experienced and **act** to make a conclusion for improvement. This allows an individual to set new targets for development or improvement at the end of the project. In your assignment, mention a traditional model of reflection and cite it as an example of reflective thinking practice. An industrial psychologist called Edwards Deming (1944) developed these reflective stages based on the work of Dewey (1933). Dewey considered that we learn in cycles in which we first experiment or experience an event, reflect, conceptualize and then try again. We are capable of mastery of our situation or emotions by moving from uncertainty to certainty by understanding our reactions, decisions and feelings towards an experience. Very often we only know what to improve after we have finished a project. Edwards Deming developed Dewey's thinking to create a model of thinking for making quality improvements on production lines: the Plan, Do, Check, Act model below.

Kolb used a similar model to illustrate how learning could be achieved by examining experience, and many students use this model in their reflective assignments (1984). Gibbs added the importance of feelings and emotions of an experience as a way to personal understanding and explanation of a situation. In writing refectively, this allows the writer to generate new ideas for improvement from the point of experience (1988).

The Plan, Do, Check, Act Model: PDCA

Plan

What do you hope to achieve by or learn from the event?

Do

What actually happened when you did something?

Were your expectations met?

What was unexpected?

How did this make you feel?

Check

What amendments or different approaches did you put in place?

Did these changes work?

Act

What would you do to change the plan for next time?

In writing reflectively, Edward Deming's Plan, Do, Check, Act model can translate into the question:

- What did I think I knew?

- What do I know now?

- How did I feel about the experience?

- What did I think would happen?

- What actually happened?

- What was the result of this?

- What would I do differently now?

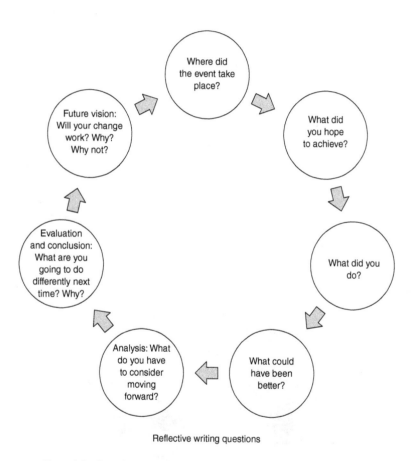

Reflective writing questions

Figure 1.2   Questions to answer in stages of a written reflective assignment

What kind of situation could I write about?

You could write about your learning environment at college or a critical experience/s or incidents at work which are memorable or relevant to discussion.

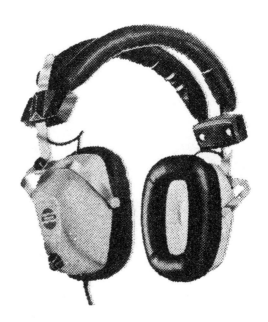

A Critical Incident

A critical incident can be a difficult learning experience which a reflective writer examines and works on logically to turn a past experience into a learning event which offers a positive new action point.

The term was developed by an aviation psychologist, John Flanagan, to come to terms with aviation accidents where 75% of cases were caused by 'human error'.

When people work together, decision making as a group can be complex and complicated. Personal circumstances, influenced by tiredness, emotional stress or psychosocial communication, can lead to a lack of self-awareness represented as the 'human factor' in a critical incident. This factor can turn well-meaning intention into, at best, an experiential learning point and, at worst, an unnecessary tragedy.

A Routine Operation

Martin Bromiley, an airline pilot whose wife died as a result of a 'human factor' during a routine day operation, suggests that all of us can learn from human weakness at critical times. In the video 'A Routine Operation', produced by the NHS, he considers, empathetically, the operating theatre staff who were unable to resuscitate his wife during what was supposed to be a routine operation (Gormley & Rogers, 2011). He suggests the staff be given a second chance to learn from their mistakes. It is a video which suggests how a lack of situational awareness at a stressful time created tunnel vision amongst those in positions of authority and how junior staff felt unable to voice their informed concerns at the time. The video is a lesson in how empathy and compassion for the self and others can be used in reflective thinking as well as the importance of recognising feelings in experience. The link for this video is in the Further reading and resources section of this book.

ACTIVITY A reflective theme for an event

Imagine yourself in a few years' time. You have achieved an academic, professional or personal goal.

Answer the questions on one or more of the following – academic, professional or personal success:

- What difficulty did you overcome?

- What mistakes did you make?

- What did you change?

- What kind of breakthroughs did you make to do this?

- Why were you successful?

- How did it make you feel?

'Progress is impossible without change and those who cannot change their minds cannot change anything'. (Shaw, 1944, p. 330)

Over the course of your **assignment**, you will:

- Relive: your experience

- Re-engage: with your feelings at the time

- Re-examine: the significance of the event

- Relate: your ideas to the theories and the arguments of others

- Redefine: reword your insight

- Record: a conclusion for improvement based on your writing

Why is a reflective learner journal useful?

10-second summary

The template provided in this section records the experience before, during and after an event to recall the feelings, narrative of events and key information.

Learning to use a reflective learner journal can help you place your feelings about events in time and context. Then you can write using hindsight to create insight. Use the journal templates provided in this section to make notes on your learning experience and dedicate time to writing your thoughts about a critical experience. Sometimes it is difficult to remember what happened, which is why this section will provide you with a guide to help develop the theme you want to write.

You may be asked to write about a placement or a 'one off' learning experience and this reflective journal will help you keep track of the everyday detail that will become a narrative to your writing later. As you make notes, you can link recently learnt theories to practice and then find supporting reading to align your notes with the learning outcomes and assignment requirements as discussed in your tutorials. As your thoughts and feelings change, you can keep track of them with the journal template in this section to build your reflective narrative.

Creating a Learner Journal

What does the contents page of my reflective learner journal look like?

- What kind of context do you need to write about?

- What happened in the critical experience?

- What do you want to learn from the experience?

- What did you feel about what happened? Why?

- What is your possible theme for reflection?

- What would you do differently next time?

- Narrative: storyboard

- New vocabulary

- Useful writers and literature

A student told us

'The tool (learner journal) was good because it made me think about what we had done in the workshop.'

Make your own learner journal template

Answer the questions below and make notes before, during and just after your learning experience.

What kind of context do you need to write about?

- Where did the learning event take place?

- How long was it?

- Who was in the event?

- How does your organization work?

- What kind of staffing was included?

- Why not make an organigram? (this is a diagram of the organizational structure of your workplace)

Make your notes here:

....

....

....

....

....

What happened in the experience?

- Were things as expected?

- What were the critical incidents?

- Did you have false expectations? Why?

- How were they different?

- What happened as you saw it?

- What happened as others saw it?

Make your notes here:

....

....

....

....

....

What do you want to learn from the experience?

- How and what will I learn in the event?

- What is my prior knowledge or experience of the event?

- What do I need to know?

- What do I want to achieve from the event?

Make your notes here:

....

....

....

....

....

How did you feel about what happened?

- **What** did you feel?

- **When** did you feel this?

- **Where** did you feel it?

- **Why** did you feel a certain way?

- **Which** actions can you link to your feelings?

- **Who** caused these feelings?

Make your notes here:

....

....

....

....

....

What is your possible theme for your experience?

- What kind of insight have you had as a result of the experience?

- Can you link your insight to a theme for reflection?

- What sort of subject theories or further reading might support this theme?

- Can you find a theory linked to your theme?

Make your notes here:

....

....

....

....

....

What would you do differently next time?

- What is your final insight or conclusion on the learning event?

- What would you like to do better next time?

- What kind of improvement could be made to the learning event or work practice?

Make your notes here:

....

....

....

....

....

Being creative can be key to your learning; whether making a summary or writing ideas, not everything has to be in black and white. Use colour or images to realize and develop your ideas.

This can release a more rewarding research time and create memorable notes:

- Write a short story of the learning event.

- Make a cartoon storyboard of events.

- Complete memorable dialogues in the cartoon.

Draw your own cartoons here:

Vocabulary

Make space in your journal for notes on new or key words. Come up with definitions of technical terms you hear or read during, after or before the learning event.

Define the words here:

....

....

....

....

Useful Writers and Literature

Keep track of writers' names, useful reports, publications and online sources. Make your notes here:

....

....

....

....

Q&A

Will my initial ideas, reflections and insights about my experience change?

Yes, researching reflectively allows you to improve your ideas about an experience.

'If no outer adventure happens to you, then no inner adventure happens to you either.'
(Jung, 1956, p. 263)

Generating Themes from Your Journal

Tales of the Unexpected

Prepare what you want to write for an academic, a professional or personal situation and be ready to make notes on the unexpected. Turn any disappointment created by any unmet expectations into a useful writing source for the critical experience.

Change your 'on the spot' failure into a reflective writing chance. Frame the tales of the unexpected into a learning opportunity to explore theory and argument. To find a good source, you may have to experience a problematic situation and turn a critical incident into a learning event.

Study Walks

Solvitar Ambulado literally means walking to solve a problem. This is a good way to think and reflect. Walking around the library oxygenating or thinking in the park can be more inspirational than staying in your comfort zone with a cup of hot chocolate and a Belgian bun. Save phrases, themes or issue ideas as they occur to you. Waiting at a bus stop or running on a treadmill, you could be struck by a lightbulb moment. Good ideas often arrive at a bad moment, so keep your journal or a 'post it' note handy for your inspiration.

Reflecting in Your Sleep

You may go to bed thinking about an event and wake up inspired with answers. Try not to do too much to load your mind in the first hour after you wake up with distractions including social media or the worsening news. The first hour awake may be a time when you are downloading key solutions to problems or incidents from yesterday. A good sleep may have helped you to unravel the tangle of ideas from the day before, so have an open mind and notepad ready for inspiration for the rise and shine time.

CHECK POINT   Learner journal assessment

You may have to present a learner journal for assessment, but no need to make your more private developmental ideas public.

You could show a tutor evidence of:

- The way you learn best or worst

- New things learnt

- Moments of breakthrough, insight or fresh perspective

- Honesty in showing your error

- Matching your journal entries with academic influences, theories, work policy or law

- Linking the content and outcomes of the journal to course objectives and learning outcomes

- Problem solving and decision making, and evidence based practice (EBP)

- Raising further research questions

- Dealing with unmet expectations or disappointment

How do I prepare for a reflective assignment?

10-second
summary

You can save yourself a lot of time and marks by asking your subject tutor and peers the right questions before you start researching and writing up a reflective assignment.

In this section, look at the questions to ask tutors in formal tutorials about language and other assignment requirements and also consider how you can meet other students to form study groups to learn socially.

The subject tutorial could be a one-to-one meeting or group tutorial. Establish a good working relationship with the person who will mark your work and discuss writing and research themes and goals. Different tutors will have different ideas about what they want from a reflective assignment.

Some tutors may want you to use the first person 'I' to express personal feelings. Other tutors may want a more objectified approach to critical incidents and use of the third person. The meaning of words like critical thinking, analysis and evaluation may be used in different ways by different tutors.

Be persistent in concept checking the learning outcomes, assignment guidelines or marking criteria. Meet your subject tutor or form a study group with other students on your course to focus and define your research question. Finding out about the assignment is a good way to learn socially. If you do not ask a simple question about the relevance of what you want to write, you may not receive a simple answer.

A student told us

'I found out in the tutorial I had to cite writers and sources in my reflective assignment.'

Getting Ready for One-to-One or Group Tutorials

The Assignment Tutorial

Meeting your subject tutor is a social opportunity and a chance to get to know someone who will help you. Smile, be friendly and ready to chat for a while about almost anything at all. This is an icebreaker and a way to clear the mind before discussing assignment-related questions. Your tutors may be authority figures on your subject area and make mental notes on your interest level and participation in the tutorial. However, do not feel intimidated as they are friendly too and also your best resource for structuring and researching your writing. A subject tutorial is your chance to process and start developing a theme, so asking questions about reading sources or possible areas of investigation is good.

You may not have to develop original insight, but you will have to bring curiosity to the party, so ask away with simple questions for simple answers. This may mean sharing your thoughts and feelings, so your tutor can act as an informative sounding board for your personal reflection, and asking questions is a standard experiential way of learning the unwritten and changing rules of researching and writing.

Make Your Own Study Group Tutorial

Why not make your own study group? Just ask some of your course members. Start socially with some basic questions about interests, background or even what the students do or did at the weekend. Learn to be socially responsible at the meeting by arriving on time and having something to say. These informal meetings are a great way to destress, so if you are not sure about something, see if any peers feel the same way.

Use an informal social media group online; try Facebook, WhatsApp or Twitter or meet in person and establish meeting times. This means you do not have to study, write or research alone; before you know it, you could be using GoogleDocs before the final deadline to share and check samples of writing.

Students should understand that they cannot copy or collude in writing as checking software (Turnitin) will automatically detect the similarity of student papers. But why work alone? After all, Beethoven did not work that way; he was sociable and regularly shared his thoughts and ideas with others. It is this social meeting which can be a spark for the synapses.

Rules for Your First Social Student Group Assignment Meeting

- Start with a chat: get to know each other
- Be friendly and open
- Find out what you do and do not know about an assignment
- Be socially responsible and on time
- Do not be too critical
- Praise others and develop suggestions
- Discuss ideas but do not copy the conclusions of others
- Arrange another meeting

What can I ask my subject tutor or my study group?

Below is a list of subject-related questions you might ask in the tutorial:

Can we use the first person?

What are the learning outcomes of this assignment?

What is the structure of the assignment?

Can we use critical thinking in a reflective assignment? How?

What kind of reading do you recommend?

What kinds of themes and theories are useful to research?

Which area of research is most interesting to you?

Imagine that you are going to meet your subject tutor or a group of students on your course to talk about the assignment. Prepare questions for your specific reflective assignment:

1

2

3

4

5

Q&A

Can I use 'I' in my reflective account?

Check with tutors if you can use the informal 'I' or whether you should use the formal passive tense, for example: 'I said something embarrassing' or 'Something embarrassing was said.'

Examples of the first person in reflection:

I felt…

I thought…

I believe…

I did not feel…

I did not think…

I did not believe…

Showing caution:

It is always worth prefacing your beliefs, views or ideas with cautious language.

Being too direct can sound like an overconfident opinion stated as fact.

Showing how you view the learning event:

This could be as a result of…

This might be because…

The reason for this could be…

This suggests…

This indicates…

Showing what you have gained:

My ability to…

My level of skills…

My knowledge of…

Showing what you can improve:

I would like to improve my understanding of…

My understanding needs improvement…

Writing your argument:

Jones demonstrates…

Jones states…

Jones argues…

Jones suggests…

Jones mentions…

Showing significance in your argument:

This is significant because…

The impact of this is…

The result illustrates…

Tip

When reporting the views of others in arguments that contrast, use weaker reporting verbs, for example 'suggests' or 'mentions' for the arguments that oppose the claim you favour. Use stronger reporting verbs, such as 'states' and 'argues', to report arguments from authors who support your contention.

Useful Words for Critical Analysis and Evaluation in Writing Reflectively:

Nouns:	Adjectives:	Linking words:	Conclusion words:
Setback	Main	However	Therefore
Concern	Significant	Yet	In conclusion
Weakness	Chief	Alternatively	As a result
Disadvantage	Major	Despite this	
Drawback	Minor	Although	
Limitation			
Strength			

'Hoping for the best, prepared for the worst and unsurprised by anything in between.' (Angelou, 1984, p.17)

What tutors usually look for in reflective assignments

- Use of correct language and style for reflective writing

- Clarity of context

- Insightful observation supported by logical theory and writers' views

- Depth of research

- Evidence of meta learning

- Honesty in self-assessment

- Admission of error where relevant

- Self-awareness and objectivity

- Evidence of critical thinking (analysis, evaluation and a conclusion)

- Evidence of use of the reflective cycle in the assignment

- Written assignment aligned to course objectives and professional goals

- Working well in a group

How do I create a good theme?

10-second
summary

By linking your feelings of an experience
to a subject that supports theory and
further study, you can create a personalized theme.

Extract key words and ideas from your reflective learner journal subject
workshops, lectures, and tutorials to develop a theme. Possible themes
are suggested in this section. Finding a theme for reflection can take a
lot of trial and error as, like a landscape artist, you may trial with several
small marques before finally choosing a scene to paint. It is best to find
a subject that you and your tutors find interesting, as this helps to maintain motivation for both parties. You may have to examine the difference
between rocks and crystals to find a diamond. As you discard and reject
ideas, record breakthroughs as moments of learning to be written up as
part of your reflection.

The narration of movement, from experience to feelings to theory, evidence and realization, requires admitting changes in your learning. A
possible theme could be realizing the difference between what you are
required to do at work and what you actually need to do. Theory, laws,
policy guidelines, and working practice can be contrasted with the reality of what you experience. This theme is a seam which can produce
specific targets for writing about. The idea of criticizing a workplace, a
learning environment or a design process may make you feel uncom-
fortable, but this criticism is often deemed necessary in the university
system where the role of the student is to challenge and problematize.
Find a way to link your feelings to a theme and then, in the next section,
start linking some theories.

A student told us

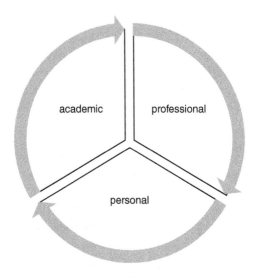

'I felt unable to contribute to group meetings and lost self-esteem, but this turned out to be a good theme for my research on how to be assertive in a positive way.'

academic

professional

personal

Figure 4.1 The general subject areas for reflection and development

How do I find a theme in my learning world?

You may have difficulties with language or with confidence in presenting, or be a visual learner, a verbalizer or more 'hands on'. Everyone has their own skills and preferences in learning. Try searching for subject-ready psychometric questionnaires or learning inventories to find out how you learn best. Metacognition and meta learning are good subject areas to help you write about the way you learn. You can write about pedagogy; the way you are being taught. You could compare and contrast your old styles of learning with the new in your experience:

Does your previous learning style fit into the new teaching methods?

Do you understand learning by experience or experiential learning?

What is difficult for you about group learning, seminars or tutorials?

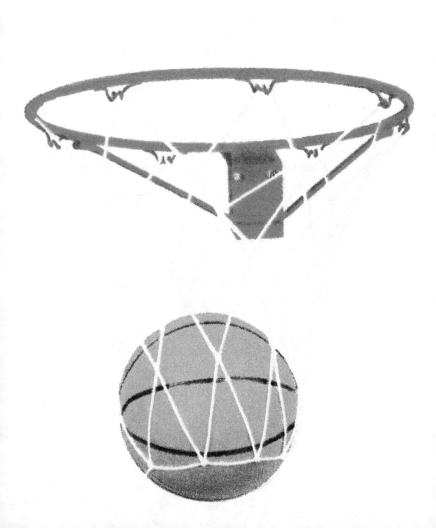

Table 4.1 Basic themes for learning development goals

Learning and Development Need	When do I want to achieve it by?	What might stop me?	How can I overcome this?	Where can I get support?	What progress have I made (include dates)?
Well-organized study plan					
Effective notes					
Critical thinking and writing skills					
Catching up on missed work					
Positive attitude to learning					
Effective revision					

The evidence-based practice (EBP) and problem-based learning (PBL) structure is common in most reflective reports and written assignments. In a placement or in an organisation; theory, professional guidelines or even laws may seem impractical, so you can use your reflective writing to prove the problem and test the solution. This could include finding a gap between work practice and work reality and examining an ethical dilemma.

Exploring the Work Practice Gap: Between Work Theory and Work Practice

The gap between work practice and work reality could be the difference between the official theoretical guidelines, policy or legislation at work and how they are interpreted and viewed at a local level. As a reflective observer, you could report on this objectively in your academic space. This reflection theme allows for professional development including personal values and ethical awareness and an informed examination of, for example, management implementation processes:

- Context

- Theory/guidelines/expected practice

- Your experience/feelings

- Cause/effect

- Problem defined

- Solution suggested

- Testing of solution based on evaluation

- Conclusion for future action

Use the light of your experience to view the personal qualities you would like to improve – for example, self-assertion or confidence building. Then link a theory to develop a framework for self-improvement and actualization (Herzberg, 1968).

Some reflective writing assignments ask for reflection on your cultural influences, or personal motivation including favoured role models. The phenomenological approach developed by Edmund Husserl suggests that your view of the world and influences are a good way to interpret and view a critical event (Moran, 2005).

Q&A

Can I find common themes for academic, professional, and personal development?

There are common themes for further discussion with your tutor or student group, and several are suggested below.

Figure 4.2 Finding a common theme for academic, professional, and personal reflection

'It is only those who do nothing that make no mistakes I suppose.' (Conrad, 1896, Pt 3, Ch 2)

Recycling Regret

A writer recently questioned the 1950s song 'Je Ne Regrette Rien'. Edith Piaf sang about starting over, stridently justifying a need to look forward not back. The writer wondered whether this was realistic as Piaf had sat through some harsh lessons in life (Pink, 2022). Frank Sinatra in 'My Way' added to Piaf's sangfroid with his positive nonchalance, singing that he had a few regrets, but thankfully they were 'too few to mention' (Anka, 1968). This defiant resilience in the face of adversity can leave reflection as unclaimed emotional baggage on the thinking carousel. It is good to avoid neurotic rumination but we all may need some regretful feelings from that suitcase for the next journey and event. An example of this is a failure to assert your knowledge or experience when at work. Use regret when writing reflectively on a personalized universal theme next time and recycle that lack of self-assertion into something you want to use positively.

Overestimation and Underestimation of Performance

False expectations are one of the best sources to use for exploring low feelings. The over- or underestimation of your own performance can result in disappointment. Those who are less skilled very often overestimate their performance (Kruger & Dunning, 1999). You may want to reflect on your abilities by reflecting on the difference between how well you thought you did something and the tangible results of how well you actually did. Watson and Glaser offer a self-learning questionnaire on the subject of estimating the efficacy of your critical thinking skills as a specific example. A written discussion on these critical thinking skills may enable you to pinpoint a particular critical skill for development (1964).

Critical Thinking in Teams

Critical thinking is a key skill of analysis and evaluation and when this is applied to decision making in a team then social interaction skills and emotional intelligence are tested too. No one does it all by themselves so you could discover a good theme by writing about your ideal team roles (Belbin, 1981).

Emotional Management

Managing your emotions at work or in college is also part of working together (Goleman, 1995) and by focusing on a particular feeling, you could use a framework of psychological theories to develop an assignment.

Personal Bias

A personal view of events can skew your problem solving and decision making if left unchecked (Kahneman, 2013). This can include confirmation bias which tends to favour decisions based on what we already know, and this bias alone may reject novel knowledge or possibilities in favour of the safe option. The sheer number of decisions we make each day are matched by many different biases, which suggests that bias is a useful theme too.

Social and Professional Pragmatics

In an increasingly complex and culturally changing world, social, professional or cultural pragmatics can be at the heart of a misunderstanding. Not knowing social, professional or cultural cues or the rules of engagement can leave you speechless at the academic party you are paying for because you simply have not been told the new rules in your environment. Find a communication or cultural adjustment theory to get you started on your reflection. This could mean writing about cultural and organizational adjustment at the same time.

Workplace Theory, Law or Guidelines

You could write about the misapplication of pettifogging guidelines or work practice rules which you believe could be improved. These may be costing time, money or upset. Your theme may include your workload or the allocation of tasks and the organization of duties. Your judgement of the situation, using knowledge or experience based on logical reflection, may seem to counter conventional wisdom, but it could be the start of a reflective theme for change and a career in research.

The Use of Technology

Looking at the way people work, learn, and interact is important. However, what kind of tools do people use or misuse at college, work or in their personal lives? The way software is applied or misapplied could be a key area of reflection, especially if there is a wastage of resources in any way. Technology may be a blessing, but it can also be a source of improvement when misapplied in over-ambitious and costly projects.

CHECK POINT — Themes to consider when writing reflectively

- Social interaction skills

- Critical thinking and writing skills

- Group or team roles

- Presentation skills

- Overestimation or underestimation of skills, talents, knowledge or performance

- Theory/guidelines/laws and working practice

- Technology

- Cultural/organizational adjustment

- Emotional management

- Personal bias

- Self-assertion skills

- Self- or situational awareness

Prioritize a point from the list that you want to put into your reflective writing. Try freely writing several sentences about the point to develop a theme. Write your theme sentences here:

....

....

....

....

....

How do I manage my research time?

10-second summary

The session guides in this research plan will get you researching and writing freely and intuitively to process and realize your reflection, using supporting academic literature.

This research technique section develops and records your ideas and provides notetaking, reading, and writing techniques to help create your personal reflective narrative. You will start by creating your own intuitive research question to develop a theme which links to your theory. Then you will be able to refine your research theme further, using a search engine and journal articles. This section suggests how to link themes to theories, using tables to note the theories and to use the differences between journal articles to define your theme. By understanding the differences between perspectives on the same issue or question, you can make your topic more specific. In this section, you can practise five-minute freewriting repetitions; and by building to 20-minute repetitions, you will develop your flow and writing ability.

As you research and write, you can record your moments of informed learning, writing reflectively and showing how you can move from one writer's view to a better perspective on a reflective research timeline.

A student told us

'I did not make a research timetable, got distracted and everything ended up a bit last minute.'

How Do I Start Writing and Researching?

In this section, a student doing the research has experienced a team meeting where not everyone gets a chance to speak or voice their views. The student reflects on her feeling that it would be better to bring the diverse and different contributions of the individual team members to the decision-making process. Using the critical experience theme of this student, look at the contents of the research plan below, then follow each session to work through the research plan to produce a focus for a final theme.

Table 5.1   A research plan to get started on writing and research for a reflective assignment

What am I doing?	Why am I doing it?	How am I doing it?	Activity: One hour
1. Intuitive writing for your Q&A	To find your theme for reflection	Freewriting: try this method to focus your theme	5 x 5-minute freewriting repetitions
2. Reading for theory	To link your theme to a theory	Supporting your feeling with valid sources	Reading in handbooks for ideas to support ideas
3. Notetaking for theory	Noting key words to use in a search to find articles	Use the template table provided in this section	Making notes in a table
4. Informed freewriting for your Q&A	With key notes you can now write for an informed focus	Extract ideas from theories to move your ideas on	5 x 5-minute freewriting repetitions
5. Search engine using key words from your Q&A	Looking for four journal articles that have your theme	Ask your librarian for the best databases to search	Spend anything from an hour or two to find key articles
6. Notetaking from journal articles	To find academic support for my ideas and feelings	Use a reading technique and a table for notes	Note down the key differences of articles in a table
7. Informed writing linking theme, theory and articles	To start the process of writing longer text for flow	Freewriting without worry about citation at this stage	Free write for 4 x 20-minute repetitions for longer samples
8. Defining your theme	Using the creative flow of ideas to finalize your theme	Editing your freewriting after each attempt	Writing a choice for improved action in a reflective practice

Session One: Intuitive Five-Minute Freewriting

After you have been to lectures, workshops, tutorials and you have recorded a learning experience, take five minutes to write your own intuitive research question and answer to help you find a theme; write without stopping and then take a break. Start by writing about the feelings in the situation you experienced – an example is the main problem experienced – and think about what the solution might be.

An example of the question and answer you could reach by freewriting is:

Q. 'How can team decision-making skills be more inclusive?'
A. 'By making each member of the team part of a decision-making process.'

Starting with an intuitive question like this provides an interim conclusion or answer which is useful for starting to define your reflective theme.

ACTIVITY

Try the five-minute intuitive writing session on the questions below:

What interests you about the experience?

What kind of feeling did you experience?

Can you relate this to a difficulty you can write about?

What were the good aspects of the experience?

What was the main difficulty with the experience?

What is the answer?

Use the questions to finish a five-minute writing session, then try the technique on the following page to use your writing as thinking to explore your idea further. Try this freewriting technique three or four times.

Write, Edit, Extract, Repeat (WEER)

Use this technique to extract a theme. This means **writing** for five minutes, **editing** and **extracting** key ideas or words and phrases, and then taking a break and **repeating**.

- **W**rite
- **E**dit
- **E**xtract
- **R**epeat

Without theoretical support, you may be presenting your opinion as a fact. Your tutor may ask where or from whom you gained your ideas to support your insight. Support your work by reading subject handbooks to find links between your ideas and theories related to your theme. The theories you want to explore may not be in your discipline area, so try using a multidisciplinary approach. You may want to write about business teamwork and explore the psychology of why people do not always work well in groups. Rest your ideas in a new theoretical framework of several related theories.

Make notes in the table on the following page, using subject handbooks on useful theories linked to your intuitive question, and use the example table provided as a template to fill in your own research table to link your theme to theory.

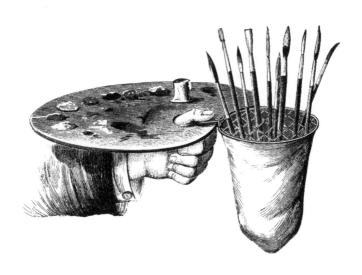

Table 5.2   A note-taking table for theories of group meeting failure

Theory	Notes: Key technical words or phrases	How do the notes on theories link to your theme?	Which themes do you need to investigate in a search engine?
1. Author: Argyris, C., & Schön, D. Source: (1978) *Organizational Learning: A theory of action perspective*	No individual representation Correct behaviour Lack of learning	Lack of open debate Defence routines No enquiry	Communication failure
2. Author: Bion, W. R. Source: (1961) *Experiences in Groups*	Pairing off Anger Blame	Dependency Fight or flight Emphasis on emotion	Lack of social awareness
3. Author: Janis, I. Source: (1982) *Groupthink*	Stereotyping Unquestioning Self-censorship	Lack of innovation Blinkered Pressure on diverse thinking	Blocked creativity

Table 5.3   A blank note-taking activity table for linking theories to a theme

Theory	Notes: Key technical words and phrases for theory	How do the notes on theories link to your theme?	Which themes do you need to investigate in a search engine?
1. Theory: Author: Source:			1. 2.
2. Theory: Author: Source:			1. 2.
3. Theory: Author: Source:			1. 2.

Session Four: Informed Freewriting

Rewrite your main research question and answer based on your new knowledge of theory. Write in several five-minute bursts without the pen leaving the paper. Repeat the WEER technique.

Refine your interim question to write a research question based on the reflection for improvement and experience you have developed for investigation:

....

....

....

....

Session Five: Informed Reading

Use a search engine to find four journal articles with titles matching or similar to your question or theme. Then read the four different answers or conclusions in the articles.

How do I find the arguments to support my conclusion?

It is always worth liaising with a subject librarian or tutor to find the best database. Try inputting your key ideas or words and phrases in a search engine to find some useful titles and different arguments and conclusions in journal articles or books. A few well-chosen articles will help you explore the differences you need to write analysis and evaluation. Spending two hours looking at the titles, abstracts, introductions and conclusions of a journal article is not a waste of time. Getting a few articles that differ in their conclusion on the same research aim is better than getting a hundred which are all the same.

Effective reading can save time. Try the technique below to make summaries of the articles.

RARR (Review, Aim, Read, Research)

Review the article title and abstract and conclusions to check the relevance to your research theme.

Aim: Write two questions on your chosen theme you hope the article will cover.

1

2

Read: Read for arguments and conclusions as answers to your aims.

Research questions: Using the main arguments and conclusions of the articles, answer the research questions.

Tip

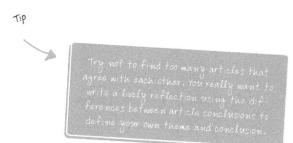

Try not to find too many articles that agree with each other. You really want to write a lively reflection using the differences between article conclusions to define your own theme and conclusion.

Do you have difficulty reading?

Many people read the same page more than once if the information is important or even badly written. Surprisingly, sitting in a busy place and reading can be good for your concentration. Your mind is a muscle and needs exercise too. The harder you work your mind to shut out the noise, the better it remembers and thinks. If the article still does nothing for you, read something more relevant or better written. Reading well-chosen articles for short periods intensively for different arguments and conclusions can save you a lot of research and writing time.

Inclusive Aids to Reading and Writing

A busy setting can be the worst place to read for some people. For those who suffer difficulties in reading, there is software to help you listen to journal articles. Cut and paste an article on the screen and listen back to it using the Word Aloud tab in the Microsoft Word Review section. By using Google Voice typing in the Tools tab of a Google doc, you can also read your ideas onto the screen. It is possible to make notes or even read your entire assignment this way.

Make notes on the differences between articles with the same aim, using the table below.

Table 5.4 A blank note-taking table for finding the differences between writers to help define your theme

Which research questions do you want to ask before reading?	What is the main research aim of the article?	What is the summary research conclusion?	Can you describe the difference between article conclusions to define a theme?	Source
1 2				Article A: Summary
1 2				Article B: Summary
1 2				Article C: Summary

Freewrite as much as you can about your assignment in 20-minute repetitions with five-minute breaks. There is no need to cite authors at this stage, as this writing is about creating a sense of cohesion and flow.

ACTIVITY

Freewrite a final conclusion for 20 minutes on the improvement or development to your critical incident or experience. You can use this as the starting point for a rough draft in the next section.

Q&A

When freewriting, should I stop to add the names of writers and other sources to my writing?

Do not stop to cite authors at this freewriting stage or worry about the correct use of language. Write for getting started, flow or even clearing your head for the rewrite.

'Not everything that is faced can be changed; but nothing can be changed until it is faced.' (Baldwin, 1962)

Milestone

Congratulations! You can now write intuitively about a personal feeling and link it to academic theories with informed reading to create a theme for reflection.

What do I need to write a rough plan?

10-second
summary

Use a generic assignment introduction
template as a rough plan for your first
reflective writing draft. Use the plan as
a basis for free-writing, thinking and
drafting your way to a deadline.

After informed reading and writing on a theme, you can now make a rough plan for your reflective assignment. A rough plan allows you to get an overview of your whole assignment. This plan can be based on a generic introduction template provided in this section. A typical introduction signposts and summarizes everything that will be in the assignment; this will include your theme and suggestions for your future development. The plan you write in this section briefly sketches out the path of reflection for your theme. This may just be an interim plan, but you can map your ideas clearly by writing and thinking them through first.

In this section, see how you can avoid the temptation of trying to start by writing the perfect introduction; instead use the introduction as a template in this section to write a rough plan. Very often, if you try to write the perfect introduction, you can suffer from uncertainty and confusion as you change the introduction to accommodate new information as you will discard many of your first thoughts in the research and drafting process and change definitions, words and phrases as you go. It is good to write your introduction last. Use the generic introduction plan at this stage as a way to point towards further research and writing.

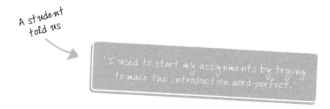

A student told us

'I used to start my assignments by trying to make the introduction word-perfect.'

What are the different parts of my rough plan?

Introductory sentences

Write a sentence/s which generally indicates the significance of the subject area that you intend to write about. An example of this is: 'Making presentations can require getting over the anxiety of speaking in front of others. Overcoming this anxiety in a groupwork situation can be a test in itself…'

Write a theme-based introductory sentence below:

....

....

....

....

Context

Your context could be your organization or placement institution and how people work or learn there. Who do you work or learn with? How is it organized? Can you place your critical incident or experience in a general or national context? You could use arguments of facts to cite statistics from reports or research.

Describe your context here:

....

....

....

....

Definition of key terms

What key technical and non-technical words will you have to define for a non-expert to help them understand your themes and context? This means that you should explain your interpretation of the key words you will use throughout your assignment. What kind of words do you need to explain or define in your own context?

Write the key words for your definition below:

....

....

....

....

Rationale

Why is your theme important?

How will your theme help you or others to learn, study or work better?

Will it challenge current academic theory or working practice?

Does it cover academic, professional or personal development?

Make notes on the importance of your rationale below:

....

....

....

....

Theme or research question for reflection

What is the theme or issue of your question and answer? This is the golden thread which runs through your assignment. It can be linked to several factors and research strands or arguments, but it should be consistent from start to finish in your assignment. Develop the words and phrases of your personal theme or issue and communicate it to others. This can be where you problematize and suggest the difficulties with a current work practice approach or working in a team, for example. This is where you can ask a question based on an issue that allows for discussion.

How can I write about feelings?

Feelings can be explored to define what it is you want to change in your academic, professional, or learning environment. Perhaps student groupwork needs addressing when you see others or yourself not being treated with respect and social responsibility. How you felt at that time can be developed into a theme or a problem that requires a solution. In the drafting process, you can put together contrasting and competing arguments to suggest an improvement in yourself or others. It does not have to be all bad though, as you could feel excited about work, study or a design opportunity and prove how your view of an experience led to a breakthrough or an insight that was proven and supported by theories and arguments.

Research answer or conclusion

In the last section, you wrote an informed conclusion based on the journal articles you selected and read. This conclusion could describe your proposal for the best way to learn from your experience to create improvement. The more specific you can make the subject, the easier it will be to write and understand.

Rewrite your conclusion here:

....

....

....

....

Outline structure

Detail the linked sub-themes you will need to explain to answer the research difficulty you encountered. Which arguments or ideas do you have to explore to prove a difficulty and test an answer?

Make notes below:

....

....

....

....

> 'It's still hard for me to have a clear mind think-
> ing on it. But it's the truth even if it didn't
> happen.' (Kesey, 1962, p. 13)

Freewriting your plan

Now you have made a rough plan, start freewriting for 30 minutes as though you are doing an essay question in an exam, without pausing or taking your pen from the paper. Study skills advice suggests working intensively for short periods. Always take a good break after each writing session and find and extract key words and phrases, and important points and write again. You may need to freshen up your mind after hard concentration before you write again so go abseiling, mountain climbing or parachuting to change your mind. If extreme sports are out of the question, then go out and get a Belgian bun. When you get back, remember WEER (Write, Extract, Edit, Repeat).

Use each session to pick out your best ideas, words and phrases or insight. All the time you write, you are refining and clarifying your ideas. This means that when you come to your final draft you can write a clearer argument. Write to clear the mind, come up with ideas and mark a path through the possibilities, trying to find the most important ideas and insights from each session.

Develop your phrases and arguments as you revise each draft. Do not worry if your first attempts at freewriting are a love poem or a shopping list; this will help clear your mind and end your procrastination guilt and just get you started.

Q&A

Do I have to worry about grammar, use of citation, language and style and structure (GULS) at this stage?

No, just work on the ideas and write for the development of ideas, flow and cohesion. You can plan time for editing a final draft when you can look out for GULS later.

There is always an uncertainty in exploring new ideas. You may not know where they will take you. However, knowing when and what you are aiming to achieve in a rough guide helps you to understand the flow of ideas and a sense of your research.

What are the components of a generic introduction?

- Introductory sentence

- Context

- Main theme or issue

- Definition of key words

- Rationale

- Theme or research question for reflection

- Research answer or conclusion

- Outline structure

How can I use critical writing in my final draft?

10-second
summary

Writing a reflective assignment can com-
bine different writing styles and argumentation to support a good idea for academic,
professional or personal development.

After making your basic plan, it is time to add evidence and arguments
from literature to your personal narrative style to create a knowledge-
able conclusion. In this section, see how you can support your story with
researched material to reach a practical conclusion on your learning. Your
personal feelings are key to developing your analytical and evaluative
critical writing in a reflective assignment. By tracing and supporting these
feelings with reasoning, you can prove, with argument and evidence, the
significance of your insights. In this section, you can learn to use academic views and argument structure to logically situate the feelings you
had about an experience. Your feelings can then be transformed into
writing and related to a non-expert reader using evidence and citation to
support the reflective proposition for change running through your work.
Try increasing your freewriting time from 20 to 30 minutes in the activity provided in this section, in which you can include the new argument
structure and evidence as you write your way to the final draft.

What a student told us

'My tutor said that my writing style was too descriptive and I needed to be more critical.'

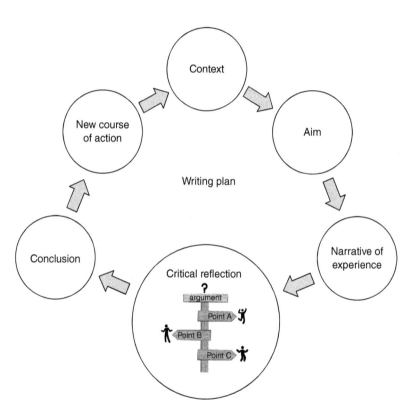

Figure 7.1   The role of critical reflection in the structure of a reflective assignment

Use the table below to consider the stages of your final draft:

Table 7.1   The phases of a written reflective assignment

Contextualize	The incident: place, people, organization, including working guidelines and practice.
Theorize	Use a basic subject handbook to find the theories which point towards your theme based on observation and feeling.
Problematize	Use different theories to define your theme as a common issue.
Factualize	Find statistics and case studies linking your experience to a universal problem.
Realize	Use language and search engines to define your problem from different sources on the same theme.
Hypothesize	Explain: what would you do differently? Use journal views to test the answer.
Actualize	Come up with some improvements for future change.

Create a themed narrative from the realization of your feelings about an experience, to reach a conclusion for future action.

How do I write a paragraph?

Q&A

How can I support a theme in a paragraph?

Look at the table below to develop a theme in a paragraph in your assignment.

Table 7.2   The key components of a paragraph

Theme or position statement	Sets out your main theme or position linked to your experienced feelings or event reality. Use cautious language to put forward your view: 'could be', 'might be'.
Explain	Define key technical terms or words to add meaning. Use citation to support descriptive explanation and facts.
Evidence	Use reporting verbs with citation to exemplify your position or insight. Cite: values of writers, research, case studies, theories or statistics.
Reasons	Develop the significance of the evidence by using reasoning, emphasis and justification to create a depth of understanding and research.
Conclusion	Shows the use of 'therefore' or 'hence' to show a new development and link to the next paragraph.

Look at the table below to see how paragraphs can be used to explore the possibilities of different perspectives and viewpoints on the validity of a theme/issue or a solution.

Table 7.3   Components for an argument of persuasion for exploring the validity of issues or solutions

An argument structure for use in written analysis or evaluation	
Theme or position paragraph	Presents and explains theme/position or insight.
Antithesis paragraph	Expressing contrast or a different perspective, this paragraph can have the same structure as above. Can start with: **However**
Rebuttal paragraph	Uses contrasting ideas, values, facts or theories to show a moment of learning to move evidence or ideas further than the antithesis paragraph. Can start with: **Yet**
Conclusion	In writing reflectively, this can suggest the new point of action you would like to initiate in your next learning experience. Can start with: **Thus**

Tip

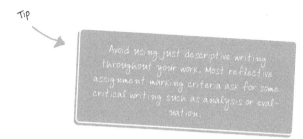

Avoid using just descriptive writing throughout your work. Most reflective assignment marking criteria ask for some critical writing such as analysis or evaluation.

How can I combine different kinds of writing and argument in my assignment?

A reflective assignment like a chapter in a dissertation can utilize different styles of writing and argument structure in a formulaic way to define problems and test solutions. See the table on the following pages to see how they might be combined.

Table 7.4 An overview of a reflective assignment, showing the structure and use of different styles of writing and argumentation

An Interim Introduction
• Signpost the route of your assignment.
• Define some technical or key words.
• Include a rationale to show why the subject is relevant.
• Add your key question for reflection and key conclusion, including a recommendation for future action.

The Main Body
• Start the main body with **descriptive writing** to set the context.
• This could be a description of the environment, the organization, the workplace.

Theoretical Basis
• Describe some key elements from your theoretical framework, as shown in Section Five, to show how you have linked your experience to theory.

Argument of Fact and Explanation
• Introduce an **argument of fact or explanation** to show how your theme is part of the real world.
• Support your argument with national statistics, official reports, laws, working guidelines or case study research.
• Stack up the facts to help define the nature of the question.

Analysis
• **Use analytical writing** with an argument of interpretation to show the competing or contrasting perceptions to help define the theme.
• Use an argument of persuasion to show the reader how you defined the theme.
• Briefly offer your conclusion or solution for future action.

Model: Draft of a Reflective Argument of Persuasion

A student rough-drafted the reflective argument below; she didn't want to stop for citation when freewriting as she felt this would impede her flow and thinking. Instead, she decided to write 'Citation needed' where she felt support was necessary. The actual citation has been added next to her notes.

Context

I felt my voice and ideas were being ignored by the group. I noticed the input of other group members went unacknowledged too. Several self-elected 'leaders' seemed to think they had to take responsibility for the decision. I thought the creativity of the group was limited as a result. After making notes and reflecting by linking theory to a writer's arguments, I decided to make the case for a meeting where everyone in the group could contribute to group decisions. I started searching in the literature for echoes of my intuitive reflection and feelings about the experience.

Structure of a Rough Draft Model of an Argument
Paragraph One

I believe individual contribution is a necessity to make the most of group creativity. A unique perspective or original thinking could be missed if this does not happen. To make this happen, some writers suggest it is necessary that all the students in the group be asked to contribute a 'what if' or testing question after the final decision has been reached. **Citation needed: (Schwenk & Valacich, 1994)**. This devil's advocacy technique allows equal opportunity for group members to have their voice heard and utilize an individual perspective to test a decision.

Paragraph Two

I understand a less structured approach using a free group discussion is an alternative to establishing my devil's advocate idea. However, the discussion or dialectic is useful for creativity if group members are skilled in asking 'dumb-smart questions', 'opposing views' or 'negative analysis' and group members understand the rules of engagement. **Citation needed (Thornton, 2011)**.

It also helps if the group is intuitive, empathetic and the members have good communication skills. We tried to use discussion techniques using thesis, antithesis and synthesis to come to a decision. This form of critical thinking could be used to explore the initial problem, the group reaction and test the solution. **Citation needed (Fox, 1977)**.

Paragraph Three

Yet unfortunately I found a self-chosen few dominated the discussion in this free form, resulting in the same people using and establishing their own rules of group engagement. Many were not familiar with turn-taking and like myself were asked to wait things out. Not everyone in the room had the same social or emotional intelligence. **Citation needed (Bernstein, 1960)**. Not everyone in the room had the same social, communication or language skills (**Citation needed**). I also found there was a lack of social responsibility and constructive criticism of the suggestions of some group members. This left many feeling on the outside of the experience when some team members dominated the meeting, 'marginalizing' others. **Citation needed (Sweeney, 2008)**.

Conclusion

I am going to ask the team to consider my devil's advocate rule for testing the final meeting decision and perhaps having a vote on the outcome. These could be an action point after our next meeting. It would give a chance for the team to form a kind of quality circle with quality questions. Team members could formulate their 'what if' question after a general discussion. **Citation needed (Schwenk & Valacich, 1994)**. It would also allow for the possibility of greater innovation as it would give a chance for all the voices at the meeting to be heard.

ACTIVITY

Free-write your own informed argument for 30 minutes.

> 'Avoid doing all writing or doing all sitting-back-thinking. And ... being caught in the middle where you write a couple of sentences and stop and wonder and worry.' (Elbow, 1998)

How can I gain critical depth in my writing?

Use Table 7.5 to explore how writers' perspectives can be juxtaposed to increase the depth of discussion and critical thinking.

Table 7.5   Using critical perspectives to gain depth of critical thinking and writing

Deeper Critical Thinking
For an added depth of criticism, use Google Scholar to find reviews that have been written by one writer about another writer. Below is part of a review of one of the writers the student cited above in her rough draft.
'As an educator in an organisational leadership graduate program, I find that my students are often interested in the practical applications of group theory and organisational theory that are grounded in empirical research supporting the practices. Professionals looking for such support won't find it and therefore may not have the confidence that the group-coaching strategies described in this book will lead to an increased team and organisational effectiveness – as intriguing as those strategies might be' (Ashauer, 2011, p.1059).
The quote above could be used as part of your argument to show how free group discussion without prior training or coaching can be an issue. To summarize: While Thornton's claims explore the analytical theory behind group coaching, Ashauer (2011) suggests there could be more scope for quantitative data in her study. If established theories are tested against current data, hard evidence can be provided. The result of using a purely theoretical framework is that group coaches may not find Thornton's ideas-based strategies are effective.

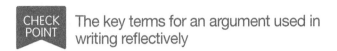

CHECK POINT
The key terms for an argument used in writing reflectively

Narrative: Your personal or generalizable account or story of an event or events which flows as a themed timeline from past experience to future action.

Issue: Main point of difficulty in the learning event for investigation and resolution

Analysis: Thinking or writing about different academic discourse to define a problem

Evaluation: Thinking or writing about the validity of different academic discourse to verify a solution

Synthesis: A thesis (claim) and an antithesis (opposite claim) can be written to reach synthesis. It can often be a conclusion.

Discussion: This is the section where the different views of writers provide possibilities and an eventual conclusion of an issue.

Conclusion: In reflective writing, this is your way forward or future action based on studying an experience or a learning event.

Which techniques
help in editing
my final draft?

10-second
summary

Use the checklist in this section to edit
your final draft and consider how talking
to others about what you have written
can improve readability.

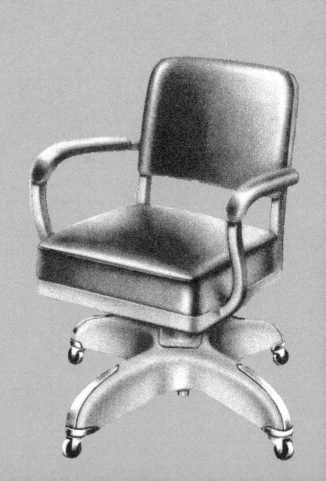

In this section, you can apply some key editing and drafting ideas. Writing an assignment is all about decision making and finalizing your ideas. Now, you have to put on an editing hat and change to a new decision-making style, so stand back from your work and judge it yourself. There may always be that dreadful feeling of having more corrections to make, so it is better to make them yourself before you hand your assignment in. If you leave it to the last minute and rush to reach a word count, your work may be wordy, informal or overly academic in places. Try to leave at least a week before your deadline for checking as even that final, final final, draft may need some last-minute work.

In this section, you will learn to move sections around to achieve cohesion and to check grammar, use of citation, language and style and structure. You will consider using software to rehearse your written assignment by listening to your work and reading it onto the screen without typing or picking up a pen.

You can also learn through social advocacy how to talk about your work, using dialogic editing with a tutor, peer or friend to verbalize what you really want to write instead of leaving it in your head. By doing a simple thing like reading your work aloud to a friend, you can even self-report errors which appear in plain sight.

'I thought what I had written was brilliant until I discussed it with some friends and realized I had not written what I wanted to.'

How do I edit my work with others?

Table 8.1   How to edit socially and reflectively

Activity	Reason	Positive Result
Ask a friend, relative, peer or tutor to read your assignment before meeting and then out loud at the meeting	Listen to the viewpoint of another on your writing	Receive general feedback on your writing
Read out loud the introduction and conclusion of the assignment to the reader	Notice your own errors in plain sight. Self-awareness and self-correction skills	Admission of error as way to checking and improvement
Summarize what you have read for the reader	Find out if the reader has the same understanding of your main point.	Finding out if you have left the main point in your thinking and understanding, but not in your writing
Ask the reader for feedback. Do they agree with your version of your meaning?	Check the reader understands your conclusion, message or meaning	Positive confrontation with the reader: note there is a difference in what you wrote and what the reader understands
Explain what you wanted to write and as you do so, note the things you missed out	This is a chance to change your introduction to sign-post the assignment and add rewrites	Exploring the differences between what you and the reader understands to improve your work
Discuss the changes with another, non-expert reader	Practice: explain complicated concepts to others	Being able to simplify complex ideas is a communication skill which will get good marks
Make notes on the errors and differences that the reader explained	Explore the differences between what you thought you had achieved and what you actually communicated	Understanding the need for creating work that is meaningful and readable for others

What are the key areas for editing?

Up until now, the emphasis has been on creating ideas and working out useful content for your reflection. Now you want to edit and rewrite to create the final draft. Use the list below to check for key corrections:

- Grammar
- Use of citation
- Language and style
- Structure
- Cohesion

Grammar, Use of Citation, Language and Style, Structure and Cohesion

1 Grammar

   Are there too many words in your sentences?

   Are they too short?

   Are you using the right tense?

2 Use of evidence and citation

   Is the evidence developing the theme?

   Are the citation style and referencing style correct?

   Are you using the right tense when writing about the work of others?

3 Language and style

   Is your writing style too wordy, academic or informal?

   Are you trying to impress as you would at an interview?

   Is your use of words more important than your ideas?

4 Structure

Is your argument entertaining different possibilities before reaching a conclusion?

Is your experience discussed and your answer tested?

Have you suggested what you would do differently next time?

5 Cohesion

Does your work flow?

Is the assignment readable for an intelligent non-expert?

Does your theme run through the assignment like a golden thread?

All of a Twist: Clarity, Depth of Research and Meaning

If your writing is a like a tangled ball of string, take your conclusion and put it at the top of a new page. Start writing and explain and develop this conclusion. You are likely to add readability when the conclusion becomes the headline statement that you explain.

Often, people only get to what they want to say right at the end of a conversation and sentences can be the same. When you edit, you may find jumbled sentences to rewrite, but, very often, by taking the object in the final clause of a sentence and making that the starting point of a rewritten sentence, you can add clarity. Or clarity is added by removing the gerunds and noun phrases at the start of a sentence as an example. This is one of the skills of writing reflectively, so give yourself some time to reflect, even when you think that what you have written cannot be bettered.

Software to Help with Learning Difficulties in Drafting and Reading

If you suffer from visual stress or reading and writing difficulties, there are other ways to write and read. Why not try listening to your text using a screen reader? There is free screen-reading software widely available which can read your electronic journal articles or your drafts back to you. This is a useful way to rehearse, test and refine your ideas. Software such as Claro and Read and Write Gold or the Read Aloud function on the Microsoft Review Tab in Word can read your work back in many different accents that do not sound too robotic.

Hearing Your Voice

If writing is a difficulty for you, it is worth speaking your text onto the screen. This is a good way to rehearse your finished draft. In the process, you can hear the timbre and sound of your own voice. This is part of how you develop voice in writing. It is your natural cadence, and personality in conversation mirrored in written form. It can be useful to verbalize your ideas to hear them clearly, and Google voice typing is a useful way to do this.

This rehearsal of ideas and words will aid drafting. Go to the Tools tab on a Google doc and activate the voice typing option. It can pick up most words and does not discriminate between accents, unlike some people.

It enables you to hear your voice and ideas in what you are going to finalize. We may well listen to the sound of our words as we write which is a bit odd considering that the words may never be broadcast. It is then possible that we perform our writing to an imaginary audience or as a form of self-talk or personal narration. This voice can help the creation and flow of ideas as sounds including alliteration or cadence improve the flow of a sentence. This talking in writing can improve flow at sentence level and add to the quality of narration in a reflective assignment.

> 'Editing means figuring out what you really mean to say, getting it clear in your head ... then getting it into the best words and throwing away the rest.' (Elbow, 1998)

Q&A

How can I improve readability?

You can often add linking sentences between key topic sentences which, before editing, look like lonely one-line paragraphs without support or explanation.

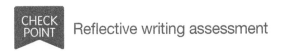
Reflective writing assessment

Does your reflective assignment meet the criteria below?

- Uses clear structure and appropriate referencing

- Identifies key issues when suggesting a solution for future learning event goals

- Utilizes evidence-based decision processes, including professional expertise, values and wishes of different parties, context and the research database

- Analyzes blocks and enablers in the learning experience and identifies how these factors influence your choice for future action

- Uses academically or professionally-credible models of reflection

Milestone

Congratulations! Now you can use a variety of techniques to research, write and edit your reflective assignment, ready for hand-in.

How do I recycle my assignment feedback?

10-second summary

After you get your assignment grade, it is time to reflect on how you did and to recycle tutor feedback comments into future learning goals. This section shows you how to start a fresh reflective cycle.

After receiving your first-grade feedback, it is time to think positively about the next assignment. The experience you have gained by writing reflectively on a learning event allows you to understand how to change up and improve things. Whether you are happy with your first grade or not, you can motivate yourself and face future difficulties with the knowledge of how your reflective writing can help you overcome setbacks, by taking a step back to reflect and change your mindset. See in this section how subject or academic skills tutor feedback can improve and develop your research and writing process and help you avoid making the same mistakes again. You can take charge of your own reflective practice, and the grade you received can be used as feed-forward that allows you to make new goals, despite the feeling of setback. This chapter shows how feedback can be a key point in the reflective cycle. Very often, just after a project is finished, we realize what we could do better next time. This section helps you to get busy researching and writing a plan for the next assignment.

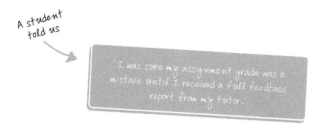

Adjustment to University Life

Moving away from home, living in a new town, learning in a new organization and a new culture are all big changes that can seem overwhelming. Give yourself a chance and do not expect immediate success. You may feel like you are gate-crashing the party you have paid for when you get your first grade back and the academic rules seem to be excluding you. Despite that shock, you are here to improve and move forward so become a reflective practitioner and change for the best.

Overcoming First Grade Shock

You may get a first-grade disappointment for your reflective assignment that makes you feel like an outsider. This is not your status for life; it is just a starting point so join in and ask questions. Jump through the tutor hoops and find the answers you need. The learning curve may be steep if you want to go up a grade and set new learning goals. Some subject tutors in departments may want to create an idea of keeping up standards. They may give low marks on the first reflective assignments to set the bar high. This can be part of organizational and cultural shock, especially as you now have the added responsibility of managing your own independent study. You may feel a sense loss of your old way of living and status. This can make you feel low for a while as you learn to manage your own timetable with none of the old guidelines. Experiential learning may mean you have to find out what to do for an assignment by asking questions. Start by making a positive research plan, and stay focused, but do not panic or over- or under-study as a result of a bad grade. Reflecting on your assignment and making it part of a reflective research strategy is a positive way to meet the challenges of a new environment. Timetable your own research and writing time hour by hour and make sure each session has a point to it.

First grade shock U curve

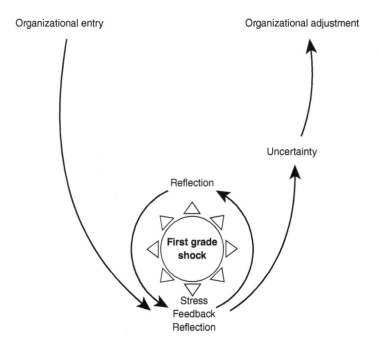

Figure 9.1   Getting over the shock of a first grade

Subject tutorial feedback session: use the ideas below to prepare questions for a feedback tutorial

- Review your marked assignment for any points needing clarification.

- Ask for an explanation of any feedback comments you do not understand.

- Make a list of learning goals for improvement with a tutor.

- Use the editing list from this study guide as a checklist for your discussion.

- Discuss any disappointment with your grade in a positive way with the tutor.

- Do not go into a feedback tutorial as a victim of bad marking.

- Aim to come away from the tutorial with some answers and action points for improvement.

Next assignment time management:

- Plan backwards at least four weeks from the next assignment deadline.

- Sit down with a weekly assignment planner which divides the day into hours.

- Choose different modules for different days.

- Make sessions no longer than an hour.

- Plan a session for a specific activity with a specific result.

- Aggregate the sessions to a cumulative goal week by week.

- Complete specific tasks for a given day.

- Get started with freewriting and thinking and reading.

- Reduce the feelings of procrastination anxiety.

- Avoid being overwhelmed by material at the start or the end of writing.

- Avoid a last-minute hand-in crisis.

'I like it when somebody gets excited about something. It's nice.' (Salinger, 1951)

CHECK POINT — Overcoming first-grade shock

- Do not isolate yourself after receiving a disappointing grade.

- Reflect positively on the difference between your expectation and reality.

- Start making research and writing timetables for modules.

- Learn socially from others who are upbeat and overcome difficulties with help.

- Actively seek help for wellbeing issues from friends or official organizations.

- Join a university club or local organization.

- Volunteer with the university or locally.

- Keep in contact with family and friends from your hometown.

- Maintain a good balance between work/study and play.

- Make a feedback tutorial with subject and academic skills.

- Use your reflective practice to prioritize learning goals.

'What is this life if, full of care, We have no time to stand and stare?' (Davies, 1911)

Q&A

How can I improve my grades as quickly as possible?

Improving reflective writing is a long-distance event, not a sprint, so pace yourself.

Congratulations: Finishing line

You can write reflectively on your academic, professional, and personal development.

You can use your intuition for developing ideas and finding sources for informed writing.

You can support a theme on a learning event with reflective models, theory, and critical thinking and writing.

You can research, think, write, and edit a written assignment, using a variety of techniques.

You can manage your expectations and set new learning goals using feed-forward.

Next steps

Look at the resources below for writing reflectively and developing your skills:

Useful Academic Style

www.phrasebank.manchester.ac.uk

Useful Synonyms When Writing

Visuwords.com

Useful Source for Arguments

https://owl.purdue.edu/owl/subject_specific_writing/writing_in_litera-ture/writing_in_literature_detailed_discussion/building_an_argument.html

Useful Source for Different Types of Argument

https://human.libretexts.org/Courses/Arapahoe_Community_College/ACC%3A_English_121-_Composition_1/06%3A_Argument_(Boy-lan_et_al)/6.4%3A_What_are_the_Different_Types_of_Argument_in_Writing

Further reading and resources

Angelou, M. (2009) *I Know Why the Caged Bird Sings*. New York: Random House.

Anka, P. (1968) *My Way*. Reprise Records.

Argyris, C. and Schön, D. (1978) *Organizational Learning: A Theory of Action Perspective*. Reading, MA: Addison Wesley.

Ashauer, S. (2011) *'Book review – Group and team coaching: The essential guide*, by C. Thornton', *Personnel Psychology*, 4(64): 1059–1063.

Baldwin, J. (1962) 'As Much Truth As One Can Bear'. New York: The New York Times Book Review.

Ball, R. and Stuart, H. (1974) *Pick Up the Pieces*. Atlantic Records.

Belbin, M. (1981) *Management Teams*. London: Heinemann.

Bernstein, B. (1960) 'Language and social class', *The British Journal of Sociology, 11*(3): 271–276. On behalf of the LSE: Wiley.

Bion, W. R. (1961) *Experiences in Groups*. London: Tavistock.

Conrad, J. (1896) *The Outcast of the Islands*. Oxford: Oxford University Press.

Davies, W. H. (1911) *Songs of Joy and Others*. London: A.C. Fifield.

Dewey, J. (1933) *How Do We Think?* Boston: DC Heath and Co.

Elbow, P. (1998) *Writing Without Teachers*. Oxford: Oxford University Press.

Ghaye, T. and Lillyman, S. (2006) *Learning Journals and Critical Incidents* (2nd ed). Dulwich: Quay Books.

Gibbs, G. (1988) *Learning By Doing: A Guide to Teaching and Learning Methods.* Oxford: Further Educational Unit, Oxford Polytechnic.

Goleman, D. (1995) *Emotional Intelligence: Why It Can Matter More than IQ*. London: Bantam Books UK.

Gormley, M. and Rogers, H. (2011) 'Just a Routine Operation', NHS Institute for Innovation and Improvement (video). Available online: https://www.youtube.com/watch?v=JzIvgtPIof4&t=4s (accessed 18 Nov 2023).

Herzberg, F. (1976) 'One more time: How do you motivate employees?,' *Job Satisfaction – A Reader*, pp. 17–32. Available at: https://doi.org/10.1007/978-1-349-02701-9_2.

Janis, I. L. (1982) *Groupthink: Psychological Studies of Policy Decisions and Fiascos*. Boston: Houghton Mifflin.

Jarupathirun, S. and Zahedi, F. (2007) 'Dialectic Decision Support Systems: Systems Design and Empirical Evaluation', *Decision Support Systems,* 43(4) 1553–1570.

Jung, C. (1956) *Symbols of Transformation*, Vol 5. London: Routledge.

Kahneman, D. (2013) *Thinking: Fast and Slow*. London: Penguin.

Kesey, K. (1962) *One Flew Over the Cuckoo's Nest*. New York: Viking Press.

Kolb, D. (1984) *Experiential Learning as the Science of Learning and Development*. Eaglewood Cliffs, NJ: Prentice Hall.

Kruger, J. and Dunning, D. (1999) 'Unskilled and unaware of it: How difficulties in recognising one's own incompetence lead to inflated self-assessments', *Journal of Personality and Social Psychology, 77*(6): 1121–1134.

Moen, R. and Norman, C. (2009) 'The History of the PDCA Cycle.' In *Proceedings of the 7th ANQ Congress*, Tokyo 2009, September 17.

Moon, J. (1999) *Learning Journals*. London: RoutledgeFalmer.

Moran, D. (2005) *Edmund Husserl: Founder of Phenomenology*. Cambridge: Polity.

Pink, D. H. (2022) *The Power of Regret*. Edinburgh: Canongate.

Rafferty, G. (1978) *Get it Right Next Time*. United Artists Records.

Rania, N., Rebora, S. and Migliorini, L. (2015) 'Team-based learning: Enhancing academic performance of psychology students', *Procedia: Social and Behavioral Sciences*, 174: 946–951.

Salinger, J. D. (1951) *The Catcher in the Rye*. New York: Little, Brown and Company.

Schwenk, C. and Valacich, J. (1994) 'Effects of devil's advocacy and dialectical inquiry on individuals versus groups: Organizational behaviour and human decision processes', 59: 210–222.

Shaw, B. S. (1944) *Everybody's Political What's What?* London: Constable.

Thornton, C. (2010) *Group and Team Coaching: The Essential Guide.* New York, London: Routledge.

Toulmin, S. (1958) *The Uses of Argument.* Cambridge: Cambridge University Press.

Vaucaire, M. (1960) *Je Ne Regrette Rien.* Green Labels.

Watson, G. and Glaser, E. (1964) *Watson-Glaser Critical Thinking Appraisal.* New York: Harcourt Brace Jovanovich.

Yung, C. (1956) *Symbols of Transformation*, Vol 5. London: Routledge.

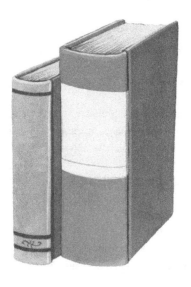